Rookie
Read-About® Geography

Looking at Maps and Globes

By Carmen Bredeson

Consultant
Nanci R. Vargus, Ed.D.
Primary Multiage Teacher
Decatur Township Schools, Indianapolis, Indiana

CP Children's Press®
A Division of Scholastic Inc.
New York   Toronto   London   Auckland   Sydney
Mexico City   New Delhi   Hong Kong
Danbury, Connecticut

Designer: Herman Adler Design
Photo Researcher: Caroline Anderson
The photo on the cover shows two children using a map and globe in a classroom.

Library of Congress Cataloging-in-Publication Data

Bredeson, Carmen.
　　Looking at maps and globes / by Carmen Bredeson.
　　　　p. cm. — (Rookie read-about geography)
　　Includes index.
　　Summary: This introductory book describes maps and globes, including the map legend, map scale, directions, equator, and North and South Poles.
　　ISBN 0-516-22351-8 (lib. bdg.)　　0-516-25982-2 (pbk.)
　　1. Maps—Juvenile literature. 2. Globes—Juvenile literature. [1. Maps.
　　2. Globes.] I. Title. II. Series.
　　GA105.6 .B75　2001
　　912—dc21
　　　　　　　　　　　　　　　　　　　　　　00-060124

Maps are flat drawings
that show us where to
find different places.

Long ago, the first maps were scratched into the dirt with a stick.

Today, most maps are
printed on paper.

A map does not show
exactly what something
looks like.

It is not like a photograph.

Maps use symbols
(SIM-buhls). Symbols
are pictures that mean
different things.

On this map, is the
symbol for mountains.
is the symbol for
a park.

Map Legend

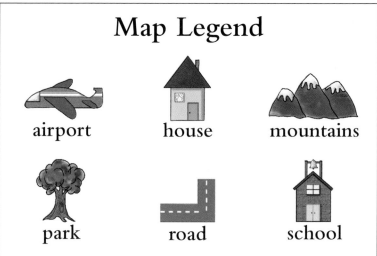

airport   house   mountains

park   road   school

The map legend (LEJ-end) shows what each symbol means.

Can you tell what the symbol for an airport is from this legend?

There are many kinds of maps. A world map shows the whole Earth. Some maps show just one town.

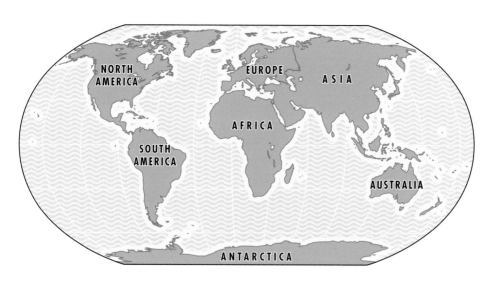

You can draw a map to
show a new friend how
to get to your house.

Road maps show us
which road to take to
get to another town.

It is hard to fold a road
map neatly!

We use the directions north, south, east, and west to read a map.

The top of a map is north. The bottom of a map is south. East is to the right. West is to the left.

North

West

East

South

one inch

Maps cannot show the real size of things.

One hundred miles on Earth might take up just one inch on a map.

The map scale shows us how many real miles are in one inch on the map.

On this scale, one inch equals one mile.

That means that every little inch on this map is really one long mile on Earth!

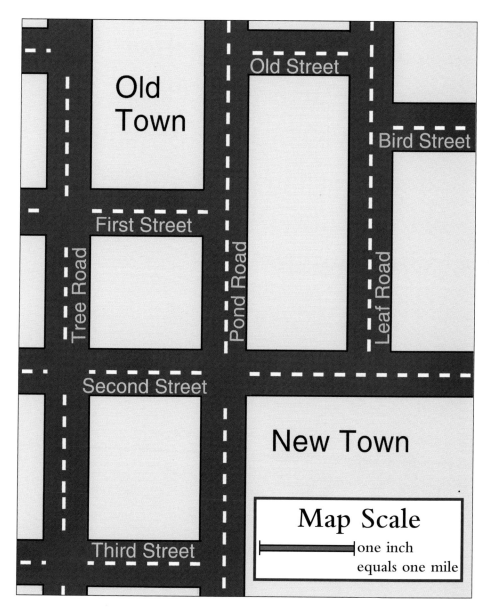

Old Town

Old Street

Bird Street

First Street

Tree Road

Pond Road

Leaf Road

Second Street

New Town

Third Street

Map Scale

one inch
equals one mile

It is hard to show the round Earth on a flat map. A flat piece of paper does not curve. A round globe shows us how the world really looks.

It curves like the Earth.

The top of the globe
shows us the part of Earth
called the North Pole.

The bottom of the globe
shows us the South Pole.

The imaginary line that wraps around the middle of the globe is called the equator (ee-KWAY-tur).

Find the United States on a globe. Is it above or below the equator?

equator

It is fun to find places on a globe. You can travel around the world with just your finger!

Words You Know

directions

equator

globe

map

airport house mountains

park road school

map legend

one inch
equals one mile

map scale

North Pole

South Pole

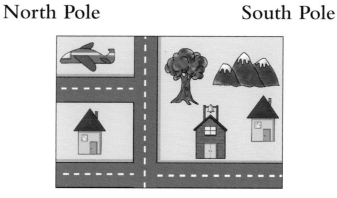

symbols

Index

About the Author

Carmen Bredeson is the author of twenty-five books for children. She lives in Texas and enjoys doing research and traveling.

Photo Credits

Photographs ©: Karen Nadalin Photography: 27, 30 top right; Nance S. Trueworthy: 4, 24, 25, 31 center right, center left; PhotoEdit: 3, 30 bottom right (Mary Kate Denny), 28 (Myrleen Ferguson), 7 (Robert Ginn), 6 (Michael Newman), cover (Jonathan Nourok); Stock Boston: 5 (Bob Daemmrich), 18 (John Elk III), 23 (NASA); Stone: 15 (Peter Correz), 22, 30 bottom left (Bob Krist).

Illustrations by A. Natacha Pimentel C.
Map by Bob Italiano.